I Want to Tell You About My Feelings

I Want to Tell You About My Feelings

Mamoru Itoh

Illustrated by Hiromi Isogawa

Translated by Leslie M. Nielsen

William Morrow and Company, Inc.   New York

It is the policy of William Morrow and Company, Inc., and its imprints
and affiliates, recognizing the importance of preserving what has been written, to
print the books we publish on acid-free paper,
and we exert our best efforts to that end.
Itō, Mamoru.
[Kono kimochi tsutaetai. English]
I want to tell you about my feelings / Mamoru Itoh ; illustrated
by Hiromi Isogawa ; translated by Leslie M. Nielsen.
p. cm.
ISBN 0-688-14630-9
1. Interpersonal communication—Juvenile literature.
2. Interpersonal relations—Juvenile literature. I. Title.
BF637 .C45I8713 1996   95–45296
150 ' .2—dc20   CIP
AC
Printed in the United States of America

First U.S. Edition

1 2 3 4 5 6 7 8 9 10

I Want to Tell You About My Feelings

"I want to tell you about my feelings."

That was how communicating began.

Communicating is like playing catch.
I throw the ball and you catch it.
Then, you throw the ball and I catch it.
And, again, I throw the ball . . .

"I want to tell you about my feelings."
That was how communicating began.
Just as we need to throw the ball
back and forth to have a game of catch,
we need to tell each other our feelings
to communicate.

If you are too close together or
if you are too far away from each other,
it's not easy to play catch.
Communicating is the same.
If you are too close or too far away from
your lover or your friend or
your child or your parents,
it's not easy to communicate.

Communication doesn't begin
with both people speaking at the
same time.
One side or the other
must make the first move.
Someone has to throw the first ball.

But you might not want to throw
the ball first—you might want to wait
for someone to throw it to you.
(Because when you throw it and no one
tries to catch it, you are unhappy.)

There are times
when you are unexpectedly rejected.

There are times when you throw the ball,
wanting to play catch with another person,
only to have that person throw it to someone else.

From an early age,

we become used to having some people not listen

to what we are saying.

"I'm busy now," they say. "We'll talk later, okay?"

So, we just wind up thinking,

"It doesn't matter what I say, anyway."

That's why

it takes courage to be the first to throw the ball.

Sometimes you finally get the courage
to throw the ball to another person
only to have him toss it away.
Has this ever happened to you?

Or you throw a ball straight from the heart,
only to have the person you threw it to *kick* it back. . . .
Has this ever happened to you?

Or you throw a ball that is a foot in diameter
but when it comes back, it is only two inches. . . .
Has this ever happened to you?

Have you ever said to yourself,
"Rather than throw the ball myself,
and be unhappy,
it's better not to throw the ball at all;
I'll wait for someone to throw it to me"?

But what if nobody throws it to you . . . ?

You aren't the only one
who is unexpectedly rejected,
who has the ball kicked back,
who is unhappy.
Maybe you kick balls sometimes too,
and make someone else unhappy,
and don't know you are doing it!

We all want to have
the balls we throw received.

We all want to have people
listen to what we are saying.

We all want people to realize
we exist.

So, who in the world is going to acknowledge
all the people who want to be acknowledged?

If the person you threw it to catches the ball you throw
from the heart, and
if you catch the ball that person throws from the heart,
then
one stage of communication is fulfilled.

But sometimes we feel,
"He didn't catch it the way I wanted him to!" Or,
"There is no way I could catch the ball he threw to me!"
We have lots of
unfulfilled communications like that.

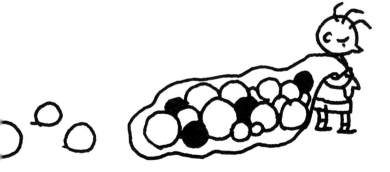

31

When unfulfilled communications accumulate,
our emotions become unstable.

We become
upset,
worried,
angry,
prejudiced,
unfriendly.

Once in a while, we explode. . . .

Then, little by little,
we get so we don't feel anything. . . .

And, sooner or later
we are all alone.

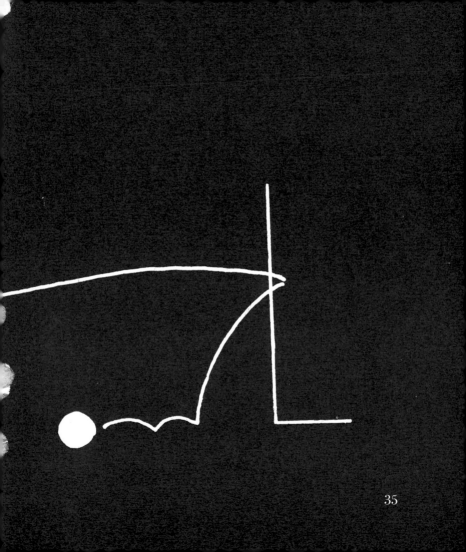

If the person to whom you threw the ball
didn't catch the ball the way you wanted,
don't blame that person.

Perhaps it's just that
he isn't very good at
playing catch.

Perhaps it's just that
he was nervous, and
his hand slipped.

Perhaps it's just that
your ball was too heavy.

If your boss or your parents or partner
never lets you have your say,
how do you feel?

If three or four balls
are thrown to you at once,
how do you feel?

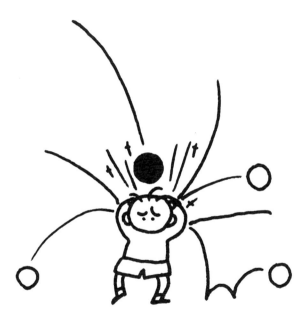

You can weigh your ability to communicate
by the reaction coming from
the person with whom you are trying to communicate.

Even if you don't want to admit it.

There is a good way and
a bad way to communicate.
To *exchange* communication
is a good way to communicate.
Not to exchange communication is
a bad way to communicate.
Equally bad is
to exchange something that is
similar to communicating—but isn't
actually communicating.

What does *similar to communicating* mean?

To talk only about the weather

or sports or the opposite sex is similar to communicating.

To talk only from your role in life

(as someone older,

as a teacher, as someone younger,

as a husband, as a wife)

is similar to communicating.

When you exchange

something similar to communicating,

you don't have to worry about

appearing lonely or feeling pain.

You don't have to worry about

sudden unexpected feelings or

arguments.

But, you also won't have the experience of sudden

and overwhelming joy—or

the feeling of really being alive.

If the behavior of the person with whom you are
communicating doesn't change
that means there isn't really any communication there.
There are only social pleasantries.
True communication
always leads to new behavior.

There is a difference between communicating with people
and simply confirming existing relationships to people.
Relationships become rigid.
Communicating can change that.

What kind of relationships
do you want to have?

One reason for problems in communicating is that
while you are saying
you want to be someone's friend
you are actually wrapped up in showing that person
that you're a little bit better than he or she is.

What kind of relationship do you want
with another person?
A one-sided relationship?
Do you want to ignore each other?
Or play dodgeball?
Or keep your feelings bottled up?

"If only I were better than that other person!" you say.

Without realizing it,

we often use communicating as a means to compete.

But bear in mind:

The fulfillment of the next stage of communication comes

with what we might call *acknowledgment*.

People change their behavior when they feel *acknowledged*.

Liking the other person is not
necessarily acknowledgment.
If there is a person
that you just don't like,
first acknowledge
the "you"
who doesn't like that person.

The degree to which
you acknowledge another person
coincides entirely with
the degree to which
you acknowledge yourself.

To acknowledge is to
listen to what another
person is saying.

"I want to talk about my feelings," you may say,
"but no one listens to me."
You aren't the only one who often
thinks this.

In fact, this is what happens every
time people try to use communication
to compete instead of to acknowledge.

As long as you think the ability
to communicate is
your ability to talk, you will never experience
a feeling of togetherness
with another person.

Your ability to communicate depends upon
your ability to get the other person
to talk—and your ability
to listen to what
that person is saying.
Listening is only listening when you hear all of what
another person is saying,
without judging, or denying,
or comparing that person to yourself.

If you are truly listening,
and if you are prepared to
acknowledge, it will be easy
for another person to speak.

Even if the ball is hard to catch, or has
been feebly thrown,
if you do your utmost to catch it . . .
you can!

You can't catch a ball
if all you do is wait.

If you are really ready to acknowledge,
take a step forward.
Use your whole body.
Stretch your hand out
and acknowledge what is right in front of you.

If you think

that acknowledging another person means

going along with everything

that person says and does,

acknowledging won't be easy.

Acknowledging means listening to
everything another person has to say
and taking what that person says at face value.

If there is acknowledging

we can have different thoughts, different interests,

different feelings—

and still be together.

When acknowledgment occurs,
another stage of communication is fulfilled.

When a stage of communication is fulfilled,
we feel a little relief.

When two people first meet, both are nervous.

The problem isn't this nervousness.

The problem comes when you try to hide it.

You are so worried about how well you throw the ball
that you ignore the worry and act like nothing is wrong.
You are so worried about how well you catch the ball
that you ignore the worry and act like nothing is wrong.

The instant you stop acting like nothing is wrong,
you acknowledge yourself.
Only after you acknowledge yourself can
true communication occur.

"I want to tell you about my feelings."
The moment you begin to feel this way,
start throwing balls that are easy to catch.

(It's impossible for a person who hasn't played catch very
much to catch fast balls and curves
even if he or she wants to.
If the person you are playing with
isn't ready to acknowledge,
throw a ball that is easy enough for that person to catch.)

73

We live by communicating.
When your communication changes
with one other person,
your relationships with everyone else
will change too.
Your relationship with your work and
your relationship with your life
will also change.
And
your relationship with yourself
will change too.

"I want to *hear* about your feelings."

That is how communicating begins.